HOW TO TEACH YOUR TEENAGER SAFE DRIVING

HOW TO TEACH YOUR TEENAGER SAFE DRIVING

PSYCHOLOGICAL AND SAFETY ASPECTS OF DRIVING, WITH ADVANCED DRIVING TECHNIQUES

YOAV AMOSI

CONTENTS

INTRODUCTION

In the guide, we define clearly the dangers facing drivers on the roads, presenting tools and methods to deal with them. The statement "I can drive correctly and still get hit by another driver" is incorrect. As you, the driver, follow the rules in the guide, you can reach your destination quickly and still avoid accidents.

Additionally, you will find in the guide that there is no direct correlation between speed and caution. A vehicle is designed to transport us, the drivers, swiftly from point to point.

Adherence to the rules in this guide will bring you, the drivers, quickly and safely towards your desired destination.

The main goal is not to hit another car and not to be hit by a car.

PRINCIPLES OF OBSERVATION

Proper observation consists of 3 parts:

1. **Long-distance observation**
2. **Eyes lead**
3. **Steering wheel direction**

1. Long-distance observation:

When observing over a long distance, two advantages are achieved:

A. Early danger detection whenever possible. In urban areas, the observation distance should be at least 200 yards, while on interurban roads, it should be 1000 yards or more.

B. Stability - The greater the distance of observation while driving, the better the stability. Similar to a cyclist learning to ride, the moment they look at the wheels, they lose their balance and fall. In a car, they won't fall, but their stability is compromised.

A longer observation distance allows for greater stability. The driver's body, their gaze, and the road create a virtual triangle, where a larger base provides the driver and his vehicle with greater stability.

The gaze must be as far ahead as possible, ideally beyond the vehicle in front. This way, if an obstacle appears in the path of the driver ahead, both can notice it together and not be surprised by a sudden stop. The advantage is having more time to react. If it's not possible to see beyond the vehicle ahead, it's necessary to slow down and increase the distance from the vehicle in front. This expands and widens the field of vision.

2. Eyes lead

This is a situation where a driver directs their gaze away from the road to any object outside their lane of travel. The eyes will continue in the direction of the gaze. Therefore, it is important to maintain a constant focus on the center of the lane being driven and not to divert attention toward objects outside the lane.

Some signs warned drivers against continuing the gaze and said: "Do not look at the view so you don't become part of it."

Be sure to focus on the center of the lane.

 On the other hand, eye lead can be used to advantage at high speeds. If planning to switch lanes, simply shift focus from the current lane to the lane you want to reach.

You must maintain passivity, and the eyes will draw you to the other lane.

3. Steering Direction

The most crucial aspect of driving requires proper steering. This means the steering wheel (not the entire vehicle) should always be oriented towards the center of the driving lane. Losing control of the steering implies the steering wheel veers off the lane, whether due to side glances or focusing on something else.

The steering wheel signifies direction, and the lane center is the goal, necessitating constant vigilance to avoid deviation. If the lane is fully or partially blocked, the steering should be adjusted to an alternate lane, ensuring it's not close to parked vehicles or other obstacles on the roadside.

Driving students and new drivers often fear that exclusively steering towards the lane center might cause them to lose a sense of the car's orientation. However, once seated in the vehicle, the brain automatically calculates dimensions.

Remember, consistent center-lane steering is the way to safe driving. Also, diverting attention from the driving lane should only occur for very brief intervals. For example, during side glances while crossing intersections or checking mirrors, it's preferable to use short glances rather than prolonged ones, which might cause a deviation from the lane without us noticing it. This means dividing attention between mirrors or side glances and maintaining steering focus on the lane center.

INTEGRATION INTO TRAFFIC IN A VEHICLE

Safety gap

The safety gap is the empty space surrounding the vehicle's body.

The lateral safety gap is the empty space surrounding the sides of the vehicle, while the frontal safety gap is the empty space surrounding the front of the vehicle, and it also depends on the field of vision. Various factors shorten the field of vision and consequently alter the frontal safety gap, such as haze, darkness, rain, and the like. When we examine the driving speed relative to the safety gap, it turns out that the equation that maintains us as drivers is:

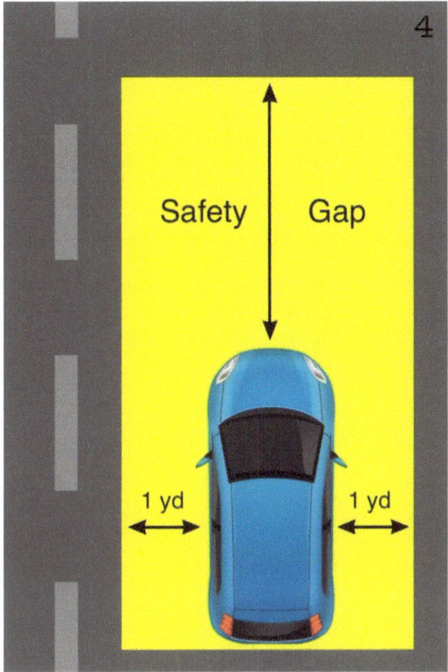

Speed = Safety Gap.

The imbalance in the aforementioned equation is the main

cause of traffic accidents. The driver must adjust his driving speed to the safety gap in the same road segment in which he drives, and it is desirable not to exceed the legal speed limit. The speeds determined by the regulations for urban and non-urban roads are generally determined and cannot perfectly express the safety gap. The contribution of the construction of new roads is mainly to increase the safety gap. Due to the growing traffic volume in the country, safety gaps are narrowing.

Therefore, we must drive in a manner adapted to the safety gap in the road segment where we are located. Remember! Driving at a speed that is not adapted to the safety gap leads to an accident, and only luck can prevent it.

What is an obstacle?

A driver planning to get from one point to another may encounter a blocked pathway. This obstruction is called an obstacle.

Obstacle = the entity blocking the pathway.

Obstacles can appear in various movable or fixed forms and can block the entire pathway or a part of it.

For example, a pedestrian crossing onto the roadway and blocking it, a vehicle stopped on the travel lane, a pile of garbage dumped onto the roadway and similar situations.

When integrating into traffic, three types of obstacles can be identified that a driver may encounter:

Distant obstacle - a distant obstacle is one that is visible from afar, for example, a parked car blocking the travel lane.

Potential (possible) obstacle - a potential obstacle can be divided into two:

- Imminent potential obstacle, for example, a pedestrian approaching the travel lane.
- Concealed potential obstacle, for example, a hidden pedestrian crossing obscured by a parked vehicle.

Sudden obstacle - a sudden obstacle appears suddenly on the driver's travel path.

1. Distant Obstacle

A distant obstacle is one that appears from a distance, and the driver has three handling options:

- **Bypass.**
- **Slowing down.**
- **Stopping.**

Bypass - Distant Obstacle:

The driver should consider bypass as the first option. When attempting to bypass, it's essential to ensure it can be safely completed. Do not attempt to bypass if there is not complete confidence that it can be done safely.

The factors that may interfere with completing the overtaking are oncoming vehicles, limited visibility, etc.

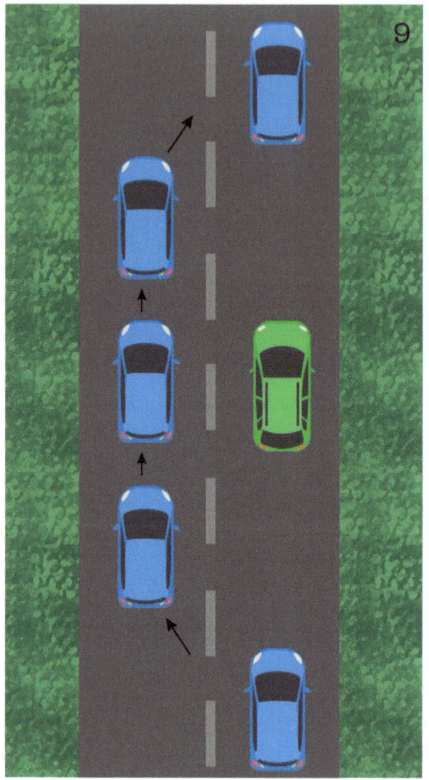

The bypass process requires:

- Check using mirrors that no vehicles are overtaking.
- Lane change signal.
- Gradual transition to the second lane.
- Overtaking the Obstacle:
- After completing the overtaking maneuver and before returning to the right lane, ensure that the overtaken obstacle is far behind, signal right, and return to the right lane.

Slowing Down:

Slowing down is required when preparing to overtake and when the obstacle ahead is preparing to clear the lane. After verifying this, reduce speed, wait until the obstacle is clear and then you can increase your speed.

During deceleration, ensure the obstacle has completely cleared the lane before accelerating.

There are situations where drivers increase speed before the obstacle has completely cleared, thinking to themselves, "By the time I reach the obstacle, it will be outside the lane."

Accidents occur when the obstacle unexpectedly returns, and in investigations after such accidents, drivers often claim, "I thought he was clearing the lane." Therefore, do not accelerate until the obstacle has completely cleared.

Stopping:

Stopping is the third option and is performed when overtaking is not possible and slowing down is insufficient. Slowing down represents an interim state until overtaking becomes feasible or the obstacle clears the lane.

Therefore, it is necessary to stop at a distance from the obstacle at least 10 yards away for three reasons:

1. Field of vision: If stopped close to the obstacle, it may obscure the visibility field, preventing safe overtaking.
2. Stopping too close to the obstacle may cause damage to the obstacle itself when attempting to overtake.
3. Stopping too close to the obstacle may block its ability to move backward or enter parking, causing inconvenience to both the driver and the obstacle.

Summary: Therefore, stop at a significant distance from the obstacle, allowing it ample maneuvering space. The waiting time for the obstacle to clear in such cases will be shorter.

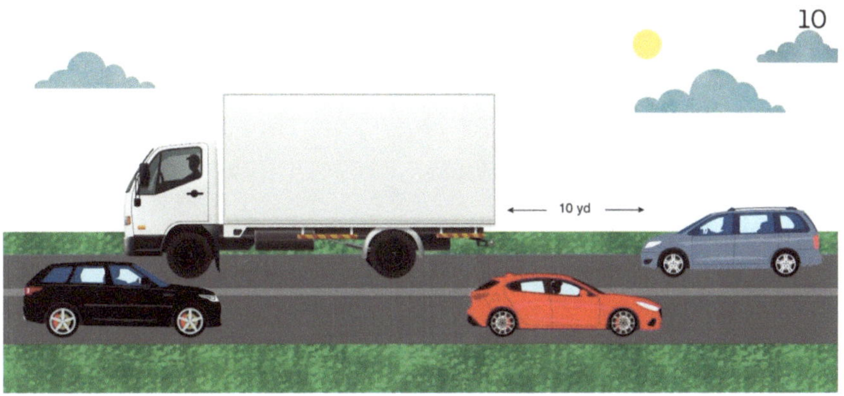

2. Potential Obstacle (Possible)

A potential obstacle is the most dangerous and lethal type. It is divided into two categories: a threatening obstacle and a hidden obstacle. Do not stop for potential obstacles, especially children, as the driver behind may not see the hidden children and could harm them.

Threatening Obstacle

Example: A pedestrian is crossing the road towards your lane. The crossing pedestrian threatens to be an obstacle. This is a type of potential threatening obstacle. In such cases, behavior should involve slowing down and cautiously passing the threatening obstacle.

Do not increase speed until the potential obstacle has moved behind.

A driver identifying a threatening obstacle automatically slows down their driving speed, whereas a pedestrian identifying an approaching vehicle slows down their walking speed. The driver, noticing the pedestrian's slow pace, may think the pedestrian is slowing down to allow them to continue driving. However, the pedestrian who noticed the driver's slowdown may think the driver is slowing down to enable them to cross the road. Consequently, a lack of understanding arises between the pedestrian and the driver. Misunderstanding can cause the driver to increase their driving speed and the pedestrian to try to cross the road. As a result, accidents occur.

Additional Example of a Potential Obstacle:

A driver approaches an intersection where they are supposed to yield. Vehicles approaching from the sides with traffic signs indicating "slow down" or "stop" are trying to cross the intersection. Regarding the driver, they are potential obstacles. He must slow down his driving speed and not accelerate until he exits the intersection and the danger is behind him.

Hidden Potential Obstacle

Hidden potential obstacles can be encountered during turns in places with limited visibility or in crowded road segments. For example, as a driver approaches a turn, a hidden obstacle might lurk beyond it. Therefore, to avoid encountering such obstacles, the driver must slow down upon entering the turn.

Under no circumstances should the driver accelerate upon exiting until ensuring the road ahead is clear of obstacles.

Another type of hidden obstacle is parked vehicles.

Parked vehicles can conceal hidden obstacles – a driver may encounter sudden door openings, a car exiting a parking spot or a pedestrian emerging from between cars. Dealing with this type of danger involves maintaining a safety cushion ranging from one and a half to two yards on urban roads lined with parked cars. This safety cushion is called a lateral safety gap. The lateral safety gap on the city road will not be greater than two yards because drivers are pushed into the gap created, and the problem repeats itself.

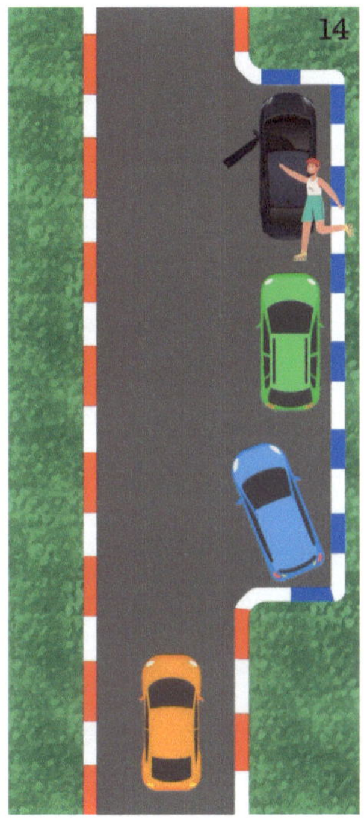

Obstacle! Door opening

Obstacle! Pedestrian emerging from between cars

Obstacle! Car exiting a parking spot

Another example of a hidden potential obstacle is an oncoming vehicle.

An oncoming vehicle is a hidden potential obstacle because it can suddenly brake, and if not careful to maintain a proper frontal safety gap, a collision may occur. The recommended frontal safety gap is double or even triple the reaction time. There are drivers who drive close to the car in front of them when they are in a hurry. There is no logic in sticking to the car in front, but if not overtaking it, it sets the driving speed, whether 100 yards or one yard away. When traveling 100 yards behind it, you arrive safely, while when stuck to the car in front, there is a high chance that you will not.

Frontal safety gap of 3 seconds

The recommended frontal safety gap should be doubled and even tripled in reaction time. The response time is the distance the vehicle travels from the moment it sees the danger until the brake pedal is pressed - the start of braking. The time is 3/4 seconds.

Overtaking when there is no full safety assurance that it can be completed safely is a gamble and a risk to the driver's and passengers' lives, as well as a risk to the approaching vehicle and its passengers.

For example, A stopping distance of 70 km/h is 43 yards, assuming the car is in 100% condition and the driver is fully concentrated. An obstacle entering the lane at a distance from the car that is less than 43 yards leaves no chance for the driver, even if they are the best driver.

Therefore, it is recommended to adjust the driving speed to the front and side safety gaps, that is, to the size of the empty area around the vehicle and the field of vision when the front gap should be doubled or tripled from the reaction time, and then there is full safety.

The law requires a one-second safety margin, assuming that the driver is fully focused. However, in reality, this is not the case. Drivers are busy talking on the phone, listening to the radio or chatting with other passengers while driving. Therefore, it is recommended to increase the margin to at least 3 seconds. There is no point in sticking to the vehicle ahead if it is too slow to overtake.

How to measure a distance of 3 seconds?

The recommended technique for measuring reaction time is to see a fixed object on the side of the road - a signpost or structure – and as soon as the vehicle ahead reaches this object, start counting: twenty-one, twenty-two, twenty-three. If, at the end of the count, you reach the fixed object, it means that the front safety gap is suitable and good.

3. Sudden obstacle

Remember! A sudden obstacle does not fall from the sky. A sudden obstacle is the result of a potential obstacle that has not been dealt with.

How do we cope?

In the event of a sudden obstacle due to distraction or any other reason, the action to be taken is emergency braking. After the vehicle has come to a near stop – if there is a danger of impact – you must steer carefully to avoid becoming a sudden obstacle to something else.

In no way should you make a sudden steer. In traffic density, this is an act of suicide.

We, as human beings, are accustomed to moving sideways when we perceive an approaching threat. We take that dangerous habit onto the road, and then when we approach danger, we automatically use the pedestrian habit – trying to steer and "escape" the obstacle. This is a much more dangerous action than the correct one. We need to get used to emergency braking and practice it several times in empty spaces so that in a real situation, the automatic response will be emergency braking and not a sudden steer. Every driver driving on the road must check for themselves to see if, at the speed at which they are driving, they will be able to overcome a sudden obstacle. Are the front and side safety gaps suitable for the speed at which they are driving?

High speed is not dangerous, but speed that is not adapted to safety gaps.

Do not be an obstacle.

The other side of integration into traffic is not to be an obstacle to another vehicle and certainly not a sudden obstacle. Places where obstacles may occur are Junctions

At the intersection, when a signpost indicates "yield", uncontrolled entry could potentially pose a hazard to another vehicle that has the right of way.

Lane Changes and Merges

When attempting to change lanes, it is necessary to check mirrors, signal, and perform a gradual transition to the desired lane.

Do not be an obstacle - Lane Changes

Exiting a parking spot

When exiting a parking spot, in order not to become an obstacle, it is essential to check mirrors, signal, exit very slowly, and not rely solely on mirror checks, but to turn the body and verify directly with eyesight.

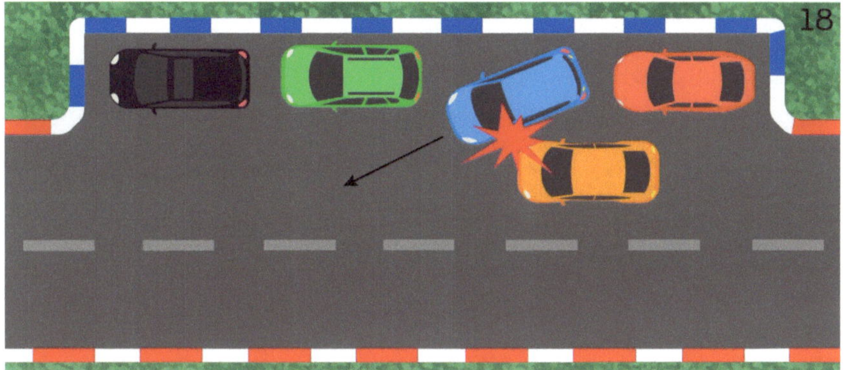

Do not be an obstacle - Exiting a parking spot

Summary

In these three situations mentioned, it is crucial to ensure that they do not become obstacles. Note that the higher the speed of the approaching vehicle, the more severe the impact will be. In fact, when you become an obstacle, you lose the ability to react and all that remains is to hope that the approaching vehicle can overcome the obstacle placed in its path. Drivers sometimes endanger themselves when they notice an approaching vehicle near a crossroads. They enter the crossroads and are confident that they will merge into traffic despite the dangerous crossing.

This is what the saying means, "Better to lose a moment in life than life in a moment."

Conclusion

If there is no full assurance that you can cross the crossroads safely, do not cross! Do not take risks! For some reason, drivers tend to be careless when changing lanes, looking in mirrors, and activating signals. In fact, there is no difference between entering a crossroad with a red light and crossing an uncontrolled lane change, because in both cases - the uncontrolled action - may pose a sudden obstacle to another vehicle and the resulting accident is inevitable.

Furthermore, in dealing with obstacles and potential obstacles, it is important to anticipate and address them: adhere to the safety gap that matches the driving speed and reduce driving speed in places where the safety gap is minimized.

CROSSING INTERSECTIONS

When approaching an intersection where you are required to yield, it's crucial to avoid becoming a sudden obstacle to vehicles with the right of way. Here are the actions you should take:

A. Look Far to the Sides:

Before entering the intersection, you must look far to the sides. If your gaze is too short, you may not notice a vehicle approaching at a distance. Your visual check should extend at least 100 yards to each side on urban roads. If visibility is limited where you are positioned, proceed cautiously until your field of vision opens to the necessary distance.

B. Check the Speed of Approaching Vehicles:

The most important thing to check when a vehicle is approaching the intersection is its speed of approach. You should glance two or three times to determine the speed of the approaching vehicle. The decision to cross the intersection or not must primarily rely on the speed of the vehicle approaching the intersection.

C. Check All Directions:

There are situations at intersections where traffic flows from one direction while there is none from another. If you only check the direction from which traffic is flowing and attempt to cross the intersection, you may be surprised by traffic from the other direction suddenly appearing. Remember, the road is not static and situations can change rapidly.

D. Slow Entry, Quick Exit:

Once you have decided to cross the intersection, make a slow entry and continue to scan the sides. This approach allows you to reconsider and stop before becoming an obstacle to an approaching vehicle if you make an incorrect entry. Remember, a quick entry is dangerous because if you make a mistake, there is no time to correct it.

When you reach the center of the intersection, quickly clear it because if a vehicle approaches while you are in the center, you should vacate the intersection promptly to avoid being an obstacle.

E. Continuous Scanning Until Exit:

Do not stop scanning the sides once you enter the

intersection; continue scanning until you exit the intersection. This allows you, as a driver, to reconsider your entry or vacate the intersection quickly.

By following these actions, you can safely navigate intersections and reduce the risk of accidents caused by sudden obstacles. Always prioritize caution and awareness when approaching and crossing intersections.

ACQUIRED HABITS BEFORE DRIVING AND THEIR RISKS TO NEW DRIVERS

A. When seated and conversing with friends, our brain automatically gauges the distance to adjust the volume of our voice accordingly. In a car, we tend to apply this habit by only focusing on distance. However, when crossing intersections, it's crucial to also consider speed.

In a recent accident, a young driver was asked why they crossed when a vehicle was approaching. His answer was I saw the vehicle, but it was far away. That is, the reference was only to the distance and the speed was not taken into account.

B. As pedestrians we naturally change direction by using our hips and legs. Whereas, when driving, changing direction is done with the hands (steering). Accidents occur when drivers, accustomed to using their legs and pressing the accelerator, inadvertently react by trying to correct the steering, often resulting in collisions with nearby trees or other vehicles. In summary, new drivers are advised to place their foot on the brake pedal rather than the accelerator, ensuring they do not press it accidentally.

C. Gazing - During leisurely walks, our pace is around 3 to 4 km/h, and our visual scanning range is typically 10 to 15 yards. However, when driving, the speed increases significantly—10 times, 20 times, or even 40 times faster than walking pace. Therefore, the visual scanning range should be adjusted accordingly.

Failing to adapt the visual scanning range to driving speeds can lead to delayed recognition of hazards. It's crucial to slow down when approaching intersections and turns and extend the visual scanning range appropriately.

Some licensed drivers fear driving due to their short-range gaze, not fully grasping the connection between fear and limited scanning ability. To address this, drivers should practice and train their eyes while driving to handle both distant and flexible visual scanning effectively.

In summary, while it's important to look as far ahead as possible while driving, it's equally crucial to maintain flexibility in visual scanning, adjusting it according to the driving conditions.

CHANGING LANES AT HIGH SPEEDS

When planning to change lanes at high speeds—whether for overtaking or turning left—it is important to use the eye lead technique (see Eye Lead chapter). To benefit from "eye lead," simply redirect your intended gaze. Avoid using your hands; maintain bodily passivity, allowing your eyes to focus on the desired lane.

Additionally, do not slow down before changing lanes; maintain your current speed. Slowing down can cause vehicles behind you to attempt overtaking, thereby preventing the lane change. However, this does not mean that slowing down is prohibited. Slowing down before changing lanes should be done when approaching an intersection or when there is heavy traffic behind you. Slow down, attempt the lane change and, importantly, avoid becoming an obstacle to other vehicles during lane changes.

Merging

Exercise caution to avoid becoming an obstacle when merging with traffic coming from behind. Therefore, ensure that your driving speed matches or is slightly higher than that of the vehicles approaching from behind. Merging onto a road when the following traffic is moving significantly faster than your own speed is highly dangerous. You may become an obstacle, potentially causing an accident due to the approaching vehicle's deviation or impacting other vehicles.

Moreover, during merges, utilize the eye lead technique. Do not cut sharply towards the lane you wish to merge into; instead, merge gradually.

POSITIONING AT INTERSECTIONS

Proper Positioning at High-Importance Intersections to Prevent Accidents. On one hand, drivers intending to cross the intersection safely must reach an optimal field of vision. On the other hand, they should be cautious not to encroach the vehicle's front end into the intersection, as it may pose an obstacle to crossing vehicles.

The safe Intersection Positioning should be:

(In the case of an intersection without traffic lights) The vehicle's front end should align with the curb, alongside the sidewalk, Whereas the crosswalk should occur behind the vehicle.

Intersection Positioning When Road Lines Are Not Aligned

But Sometimes the road lines are not aligned (see Illustration). In such cases, position yourself alongside the nearest curb—on the right side next to the right curb or on the left side next to the left curb.

Location at an intersection when the crosswalk is adjacent to the intersection

When positioning at an intersection to cross (an intersection without traffic lights), and the crosswalk is close to the intersection (see Illustration), you should align your vehicle so that the rear part is over the crossing point, not the front part. Why? When the rear part of your vehicle is over the pedestrian crossing, pedestrians will walk behind it, whereas if the front part is over the crossing (see Illustration 2), pedestrians will walk in front.

A driver focused on checking the left side of the intersection and waiting to cross might not notice pedestrians starting to cross during the intersection. Therefore, as drivers, if you see pedestrians crossing from the front (at an intersection without lights), allow them to cross first, then proceed and "encourage" the pedestrians to walk behind to prevent accidents and unnecessary delays during the crossing.

Correct

Incorrect

ATTENTION DEFICIT AND HYPERACTIVITY

Young people are suffering from Attention Deficit Hyperactivity Disorder (ADHD) and others who are hyperactive. Those with ADHD lose concentration and disconnect from what is happening while driving. They lack a planning sequence and may encounter dangerous situations or react to them late.

Hyperactive individuals exhibit impulsive behavior and may enter into dangerous situations without control. The best method to maintain concentration and avoid uncontrolled entry into dangerous situations is to talk to oneself and ask in a sequence: What do I have ahead on the road? Traffic light. Pedestrian crossing. Obstacle. And what am I supposed to do as a driver? Proceed step by step.

This means adding another element besides the eyes and brain, which is talking to oneself to help maintain a high level of concentration so that their thoughts do not wander. They will not perform risky actions and will also be more aware of what is happening on the road ahead of them.

This approach is recommended for all driving students during driving exams and for new drivers taking their first steps on the road.

TURNS AND LANES PLANNING

Advanced planning of turns and lanes is a crucial part of driving. Arriving from point to point safely depends more on the quality of lane planning and the planning distance rather than driving speed.

Planning for a greater distance allows you to choose the correct lane and avoid getting stuck behind "obstacles" unnecessarily. Some drivers, when exiting a turn or intersection, rush to step on the accelerator before planning their driving lane, often finding themselves stuck behind obstacles in desperate attempts to extricate themselves. If they had planned ahead, their arrival speed at the desired point would have been faster and less frustrating.

In turn planning, it's important to note that no turn is similar to another, and unplanned turns will lead to mistakes.

For example, when making a right turn with a "close obstacle," there's no need to enter the right lane but rather to bypass the obstacle, also, when approaching an intersection where, in addition to turn planning, there's also a crosswalk plan the turn first and then plan the crossing of the intersection.

When exiting a turn or intersection, plan the continuation of the lane.

Execution Method in Lane Planning

Remember that the "home" lane is the right lane. The use of the left lane is intended for overtaking or turning left or if otherwise indicated on the road (arrows). In lane planning, it is mandatory to consider the safety gap.

Do not plan a lane without a "safety gap." When exiting from the right lane for overtaking, plan in advance to return to the "home" lane, which is the right lane, even if temporarily bypassing several "obstacles." Delays in returning to the right lane may cause complications and difficulty in returning to the right lane.

When approaching a turn, sketch an imaginary line in the center of the planned driving lane beforehand and then ensure the steering wheel moves forward on the imaginary line drawn in advance. When exiting an intersection, and even before a crosswalk, it is important to adhere to the sketched line and continue to imagine beyond the intersection. The quality of planning depends on the length of the sketched line ahead of the driver. Maintain a sequence in the planning segment by segment without interruption. The longer the planning range, the better. Remember that driving ability is measured by the planning sequence and planning range.

A planned lane is not necessarily the lane marked on the road. A planned lane must include a safety gap even if it deviates from the marked lane.

Key Points in Early Planning of Turns and Lanes

1. When preparing to cross an intersection and make a turn during the crossing, prioritize planning the turn first and then plan the crossing of the intersection.
2. Plan for as great a distance as possible.
3. Maintain the steering wheel in the center of the planned lane.

Planning is personal—do not rely on another driver's planning.

Executing Right Turns - Two-Way Road

Right Turn

Right turns should be executed from the right lane to the right lane. Before making a right turn, position yourself at an angle toward the lane you are entering (see Illustration 1).

23

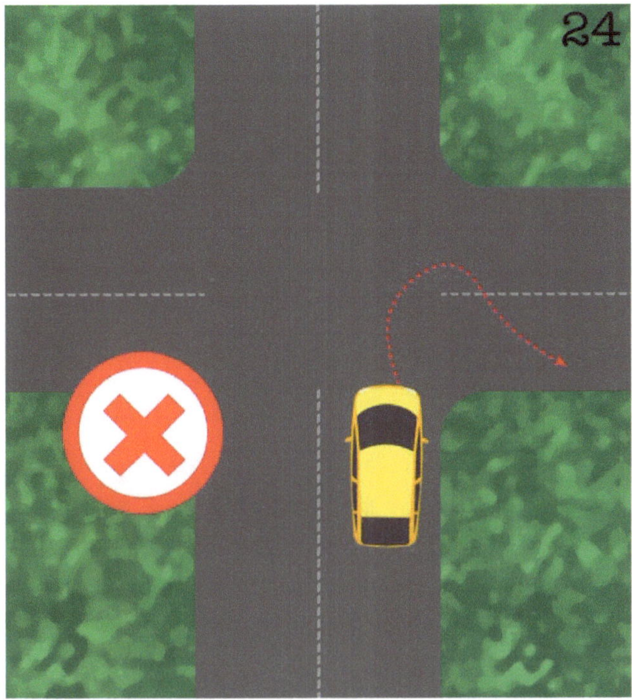

This angle allows a smooth and precise entry into the right lane. Entering the right lane in a straight line will result in a wide turn and may push the vehicle into the second lane (see Illustration 2), which could lead to colliding with a vehicle in the second lane.

Right Turn with Close Obstacle (Less than 50 Yards) on a Two-Way Road

When making a right turn with a close obstacle ahead, the turn should be planned as follows: enter the left lane (see Illustration), no signaling is necessary, but pay attention and be cautious of oncoming traffic. If a vehicle approaches from the opposite direction, wait behind the "obstacle" with the vehicle facing toward the left lane.

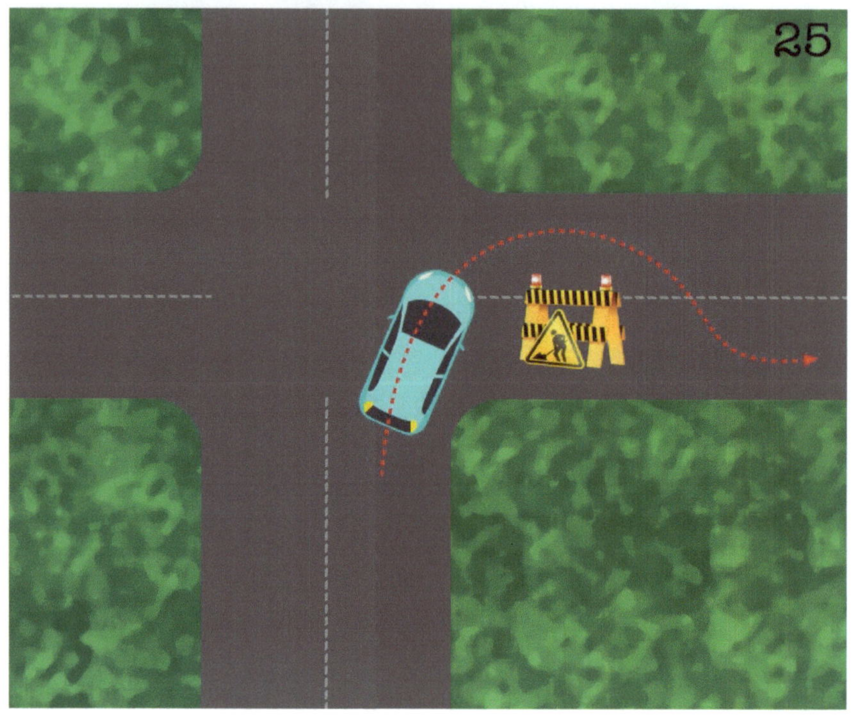

Right Turn with Distant Obstacle (More than 50 Yards) on a Two-Way Road

When making a right turn with a distant obstacle ahead, the turn should be planned as follows: enter the right lane (see Illustration) upon completing the turn and after aligning properly.

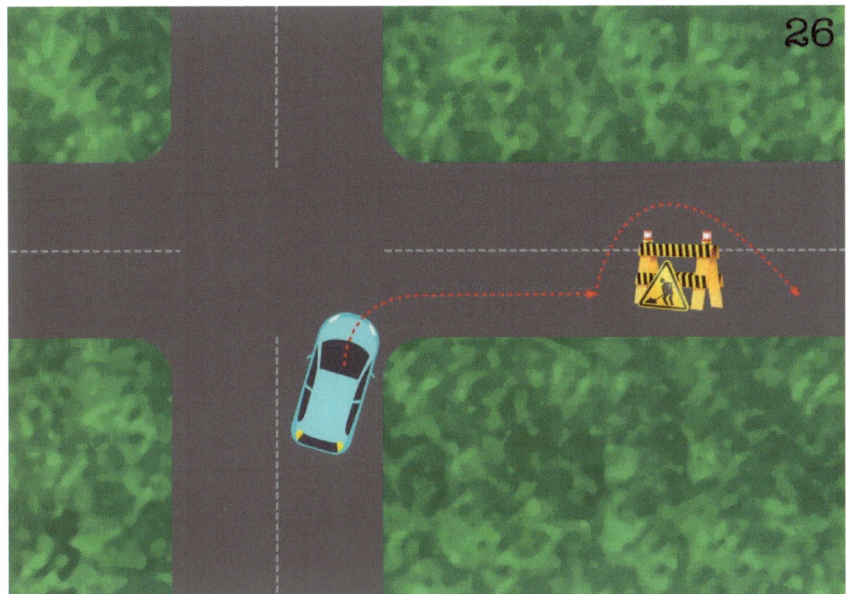

Proceed to circumvent the obstacle, ensuring there is no oncoming traffic.

Making a Right Turn with an Obstacle Before the Turn

When there is an obstacle before making a right turn, it's important to bypass the obstacle without "cutting in" into the right lane after the bypass. Instead, gradually and diagonally return towards the right turn angle (see Illustration).

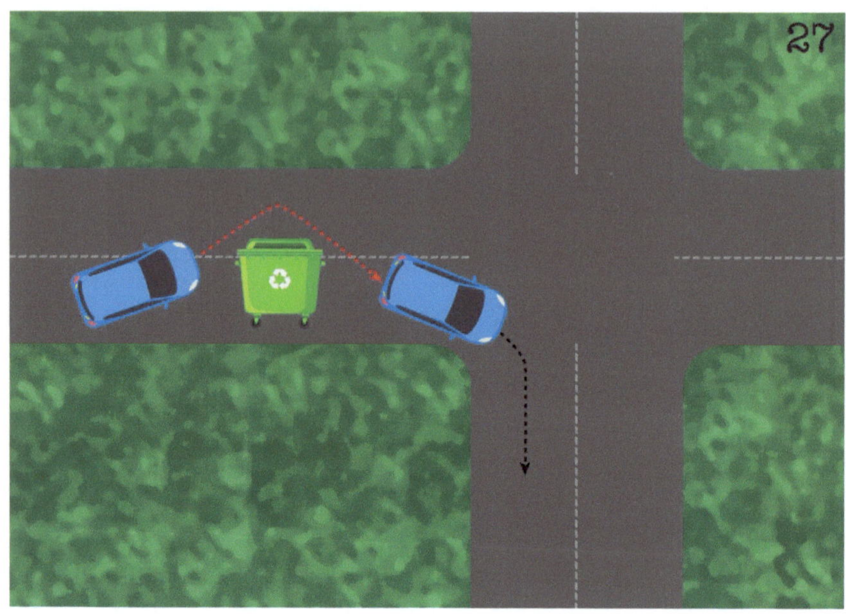

Executing Left Turns (on a Two-Way Road)

In planning a left turn it is mandatory to execute the turn in a wide arc without cutting into the turn. To do so, when making a left turn, position yourself and enter the intersection in a straight line. Under no circumstances should you position at a left angle for three reasons (see Illustration):

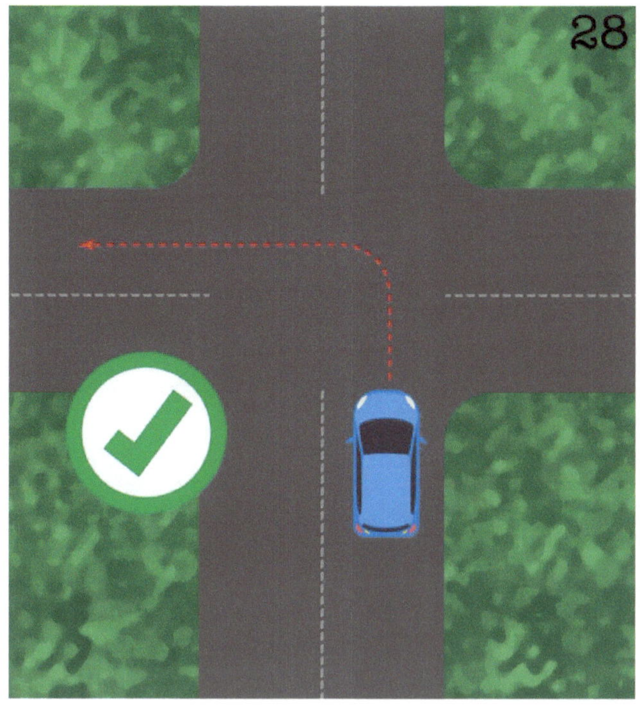
28

A. positioning at an angle may cause the vehicle to invade the opposing lane and block its movement.

B. Positioning at an angle will limit the field of vision to the right side of the intersection because the driver positions himself with his back turned to traffic on the right.

Left Turn with Close-Distant Obstacle

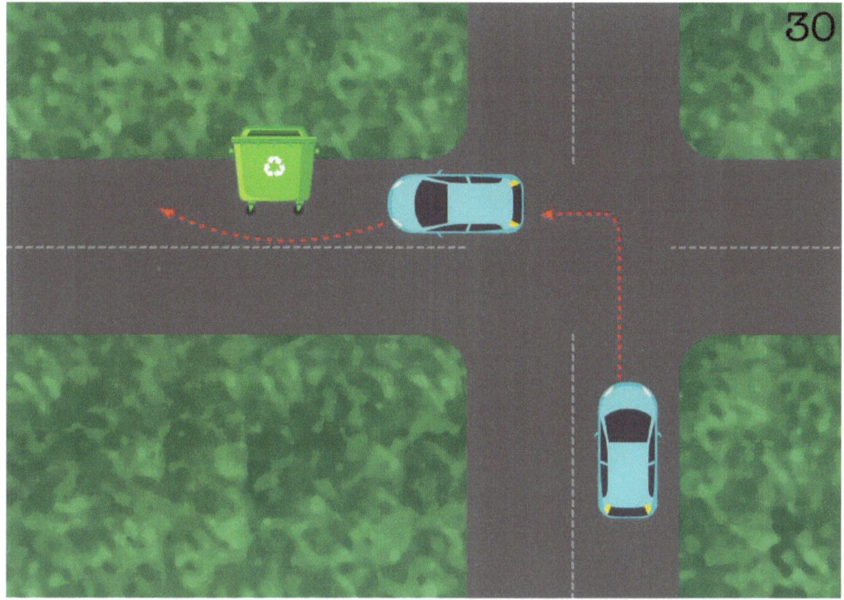

In planning a left turn with a close obstacle (see Illustration), do not attempt to circumvent the obstacle while crossing the intersection; instead, wait behind the obstacle. If the opposite road is clear, proceed to make the turn; if not, wait behind the obstacle until the road clears. This action should also be taken in the case of a distant obstacle.

Planning a Left Turn with an Obstacle Before the Turn

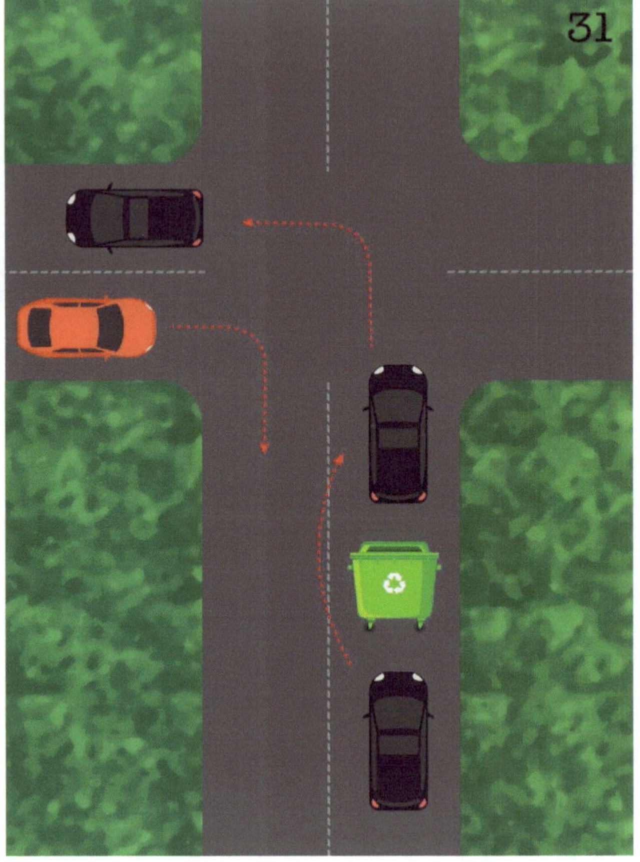

In planning a left turn with an obstacle before the turn (see Illustration), return to the right lane after bypassing the obstacle, despite its proximity to the intersection.

The danger is that a vehicle approaching from the left and intending to turn right may not notice the vehicle turning left, as the driver is focused on checking the left side and may not anticipate a vehicle approaching in the opposite lane. Additionally, double-check the mirrors before turning to ensure that the following vehicle notices the turning vehicle and does not attempt to overtake it.

ABOUT THE AUTHOR

The author is a qualified driving instructor with over 30 years of experience managing a professional driving school. As an advanced driving instructor, he specialized in techniques akin to auto racing. He has also studied the psychology of human motor coordination. He lectures to young people before they reach driving age on the psychological and safety aspects of driving.